A Place
To Belong

by Lynda T. Boardman

BEACON HILL PRESS
OF KANSAS CITY

Printed in the United States of America

ISBN 978-0-8341-3470-6

Cover Design: Nick Wanserski
Illustrator: Nick Wanserski
Interior Design: Sharon Page
Editor: William Rolfe

Author's Note: This is an All-reader NMI children's book for 2015-16. A few years after Yuri and Olga became Christians in 1992, God called them into ministry. They accepted the call to pastor a Church of the Nazarene in Southern Russia. With five biological children, they followed God's direction to adopt seven children. The book is part of the *Kidz Passport to Missions* curriculum.

10 9 8 7 6 5 4 3 2 1

Contents

Acknowledgments

A few years after Yuri and Olga became Christians in 1992, God called them into ministry. They accepted the call to pastor a Church of the Nazarene in Southern Russia. With five biological children, they followed God's direction to adopt seven children. Thank you to this family for their dedication to obey and serve God.

Special Thanks

Thank you to Trino Jara, Eurasia Compassionate Ministries, who recommended this story. Special thanks to Sasha Lyansberg for telling the story of her family that made this book possible. I also thank those who have reached out in love and adopted a child. May every child around the world find love and acceptance in a Christian home.

1
New Year's Celebration

"I love my nesting baby dolls," said seven-year-old Sasha [SAH-shuh]. "I think the biggest one is the mother and the four little ones are her daughters. I like to hold them and feel the smooth, shiny paint. The bright red and green clothes are so pretty. Do they look like me? They have blond hair and dark eyes like mine.

"Yes," answered Momma. "Even their rosy cheeks and lips look like you."

"Thank you, Momma. This was the best gift ever!" exclaimed Sasha.

"Timothy, what's the matter?" Momma asked as she picked up her one-year-old son.

"Maybe he wants his teddy bear," said Dimitrii [dee-MEE-tree]. "Here Timothy, you play with the teddy bear. I'm too big for teddy bears. I like my wooden horse. I like the way his legs move when I make him run," said the nine-year-old.

"We had a great celebration this year," said Papa. Now it's time to thank God for His blessings. "Let's sit around the tree and pray."

"We had a great celebration this year," said Papa. Now it's time to thank God for His blessings. "Let's sit around the Christmas tree and pray."

Momma felt tears roll down her cheeks as she prayed, "Thank You, God, for my loving husband and five wonderful children. Help our family to love the children of this village and give them a place to belong."

Next, Papa prayed, "Thank You, God, for this year and the special times we've had together. Thank You for our church, our home, and our family. In Jesus' name, we pray. Amen."

"Dimitrii and Sasha. I'll tuck you into bed while Momma puts Timothy to bed."

"Goodnight," said Papa and Momma as they walked back into the living room.

"Yuri [YOOR-ee]," said Olga [OHL-gu]. "I've been thinking and praying about something. Could we talk about it?"

"Sure," answered Yuri. "The children are in bed. Let's go into the kitchen where it's warm. It's so cold here in Russia [RUHSS-uh]. The snow is piled so high around our house it is almost to the roof."

Olga looked at the frosty windows as she sat down near the fire. "We have two grown children who now live in other cities. We, also, have three beautiful children who live with us. They have a loving home and a caring church," began Olga. "All around are children who don't have these blessings."

"I know," said Yuri. "That's why I want our church to help meet the needs of children in our village. We visit and take clothes and food to some of them now."

"That's right." said Olga. "Our church helps, and I'm thankful for that. But, I feel God wants our family to do more."

"What more can we do?" asked Yuri.

"As I read the Bible and prayed, my thoughts turned to children here in South Russia [RUHSS-uh] whose lives we could bless." Olga replied.

"What are you thinking?" asked Yuri.

Olga continued, "Recently, our family celebrated Jesus' birthday. Tonight, we finished our three-week New Year's celebration. Wouldn't it be great for other children to have those blessings, too?"

"Yes, but how can that happen?" asked Yuri.

"Next New Year's Day will be in 2000. Since that is the beginning of a new century, I'd like to do something new. How would you feel about inviting a child who wouldn't have a celebration to come to our house?" asked Olga.

"Wow," said Yuri. "That would change our celebration! Let's pray about this for a few days and then ask Dimitrii and Sasha what they think."

2
A Miracle

"You mean I might have a girl stay in my room with me?" asked Sasha.

"We don't know," answered Momma. "It might be a girl, or it might be a boy. Or, it might be both."

"Dimitrii, what do you think?" Papa asked.

"How long would they be here?" asked Dimitrii.

"We thought it'd be nice to have someone here next Christmas and New Year's to celebrate with our family," answered Momma.

"That's a long time from now," said Dimitrii. That's a whole year!"

"That's right," said Papa. "It'll take some time to find a child to invite. Also, we want the child to be here for our celebrations next year."

"We want to share our home and family with someone who doesn't have those blessings," said Momma. "Also, we want you two to feel good about this and help with the planning."

"I think it'd be fun to have a girl," said Sasha.

"I'd rather have a boy," said Dimitrii.

"We'll have to wait and see," said Papa.

❊ ❊ ❊

One day a few weeks later, Dimitrii called, "Momma, come quickly. Listen to our president."

With eyes glued to the television, Dimitrii listened to the president. "What did he say?" Momma asked.

"He said there are many children in Russian orphanages. He asked people to think about taking some of these children into their homes," Dimitrii replied.

"Dimitrii! God's at work. I know this is His plan for our family," said Momma.

"What is an orphanage [OR-fan-ij]?" asked Dimitrii.

"An orphanage is a home for children who don't have a home with their parents," answered Momma. "I'll call the orphanage tomorrow."

Ring, ring, ring! "Hello," answered a woman.

Olga began to speak, "Yesterday, the president asked for people to help with children in the orphanages. My family would like to have a child come to our home for New Year's."

"Come fill out an application, and we'll put it in our files," said the woman.

"I'll come tomorrow," said Olga.

"Goodbye," said the woman.

"Thank you," replied Olga.

Since Yuri and Olga did not have a car, Olga asked a friend to take her.

"I'm here to complete the application to have a child visit our home for New Year's," said Olga.

"Please be seated, and I'll get the papers," said the woman.

Olga handed the completed application back to the woman. "When will we know the child's name?"

"We'll call you," the woman answered.

* * *

Back home, Olga began to pray and wait.

"Have you heard from the orphanage?" Yuri asked.

Olga replied, "No. I've waited two months with no word. I'm going to call them."

Olga waited nervously as the telephone rang. "Hello," answered the woman.

"I'd like to know if we'll have a child who can visit our home for the New Year's holiday," Olga said.

"You are new to our area. I don't think we have a child for you at this time. Thank you for calling," the woman replied.

❊ ❊ ❊

Over the next seven months, Olga continued to pray and call. "I don't believe they trust me," Olga thought.

"Dear God, I know you wanted us to do this. Please work out the details to make it possible for this year," she prayed.

Olga stood at the window and looked out at the crisp snow. She shivered as she turned to walk closer to the fire. "This is December," she sobbed. "Will it ever happen?"

Suddenly, she felt God telling her to call again. She prayed as she walked to the telephone.

"I think there's a possibility for you," said the woman. "There are two children who've been in the hospital for three months. They need to move to the orphanage, but they're not well enough. Their father drinks too much to have the children, and we can't find the mother. Would you be interested in taking them from the hospital to your home for the three weeks of the New Year's celebration?"

"Oh, yes!" answered Olga. "When can we pick them up?"

"I'll send the paper work over to the hospital soon. You can pick them up on December 24," the woman replied.

"Thank you so much. Are they girls or boys?" Olga asked.

"One is Viktoria [vik-TOHR-ree-uh], a six-year-old girl. The other one is Evgenii [ew-GEEN-ee], a four-year-old boy," said the woman.

"That's perfect. It's a miracle!" exclaimed.

3

Room for Four More

"There's so much to do and so little time. We have three weeks to prepare," Momma said.

The smell of fresh baked cookies filled the kitchen. The family discussed where the children would sleep in their crowded house. Dimitrii and Sasha made small gifts for the children. Since they had no transportation, Momma made arrangements to hire a car to take them to the hospital on December 24.

✳ ✳ ✳

On the way to the hospital, Sasha exclaimed, "I'm so excited to see Viktoria!" She's six, and I'm eight, so we can play together."

"Well, I wish Evgenii was older. I'm 10, so a four-year-old seems like a baby," complained Dimitrii.

"Just remember," reminded Momma, "these children have been in the hospital for three months. They were very sick and haven't grown like you two."

The car stopped, and the family moved quietly to the sidewalk. Suddenly, they felt overcome with what they would face inside the hospital. Papa said, "Let's pray for God's help. God, we know You want us to help these children. You know we don't feel ready for this assignment, but we know You'll help us. Thank You for these children and our family. Bless our time together. Amen."

"You know the children are small for their ages, and they can't talk," said the nurse as she led the family down the hospital hallway.

"We'll take good care of them," said Momma.

"They can't stay here any longer, and they don't have the right papers to transfer them to the orphanage. Your home was the only choice," the nurse explained.

Momma and Papa looked at each other. "This was the reason they could have the children visit," they thought. But whatever reason, they felt thankful for the miracle.

"They look like babies," Sasha whispered to Momma. "The girl isn't even half my size."

"That boy looks like he's a one-year-old," Dimitrii declared loudly.

"Sh-sh-sh," motioned Papa.

"They're all ready to go," said the nurse. "Enjoy your celebration."

"Thank you," said Momma as she picked up Evgenii.

"Come," said Papa, "I'll carry you, Viktoria."

The children wide-eyed with fear looked back at the nurse. The nurse nodded her head letting the children know everything was fine.

❊ ❊ ❊

"I can see the children changing," said Momma after the New Year's celebration. "They are eating and beginning to say a few words."

"Yes," answered Papa. "They both call you Momma. Are you thinking of keeping them?"

"They have no other place to go," answered Momma. "I do love them, and they need a place to belong. I know God brought them to us."

"Two things must happen before we can keep the children. The courts must approve our request, and the father must approve in court," said Papa.

A year and another New Year's celebration passed before they received all the papers with the approval to adopt Viktoria and Evgenii.

❈ ❈ ❈

"You know what happened today?" asked Momma.

"What happened?" asked Papa.

"I talked to the lady at the orphanage in the next village. I asked her if I could come and help with the children there. She was happy I wanted to help and told me to come anytime," Momma said.

"That's wonderful," said Papa. "That's certainly an answer to prayer.

❈ ❈ ❈

On a cold January day a few weeks later, the whole family went to the orphanage to help.

"Why are the children going barefoot on such a cold day?" Momma asked.

"They don't have any shoes," answered a 15-year-old girl.

"I'm going to see what I can do to get shoes for these children," Momma said. She knew her family did not have the money. Papa worked very hard to have clothes and food for them. Their church was small and did not have money to buy shoes for 120 children at the orphanage. But Momma had a plan.

"Hello, is this the Church of the Nazarene in Volvograd [VOHL-gah-grad]?" Momma asked.

"Yes," said the pastor.

"I'm helping at an orphanage. There're 120 children and none of them has shoes. Do you think your church could help?" asked Momma.

"I'll see what I can do," answered the pastor.

Soon 120 pairs of shoes arrived at the orphanage. It was another miracle and answer to pray.

Each New Year's Olga and Yuri would invite several children to come home to celebrate.

"I'd like for you to come to my house for New Year's," Momma said to the 15-year-old girl she met the first day she worked.

"Oh, I'd love that," she answered.

✳ ✳ ✳

"What a fun time," laughed Sasha. "I like the children visiting us for New Year's."

"Thank you for doing this," said the 15-year-old girl with tears in her eyes.

"What's wrong?" asked Momma. "Aren't you having a good time?"

"Oh, yes," the girl said sadly. "It's not that."

"What is it?" asked Momma.

"I'd like to see my younger brother and sisters. I wish they were here." The girl continued.

"Where are they?" asked Momma.

"There're nine children in my family. My mother died at the birth of the youngest. My father couldn't take care of us, so we are all in different orphanages," the girl replied.

"Do you know where? asked Momma.

"No. I think it's a long trip. They didn't do well in school, and they took them away," she answered through her tears.

"How old are they?" Momma asked.

The girl replied, "My brother is 10, and one of my sisters is 11. I've twin sisters who are eight."

"I don't know what I can do, but I'll try to find them," said Momma.

"God, I'll need Your help. Please help me to find these precious children and bring their family back together," Momma prayed silently.

"How do you think you can find them?" Papa asked.

"I'll start at this orphanage and do research to try to find where they moved," Momma answered.

❋ ❋ ❋

"Clickity, clickity, clack," the train wheels turned taking them miles from home. Papa and Momma sat in silence lost in their own thoughts. "What would they find at the end of this trip?" They knew there were four children in three orphanages lonely, afraid, and feeling unloved.

The train whistle broke into their thoughts. This is it. This is the first stop on this search.

"Over here!" the man called to them as they stepped from the train.

4
Then There
Were Twelve

"Yes, two of the children you're looking for live here," said the woman behind the desk. "Why do you want to find them?"

"We know their older sister," said Papa. "We'd like to adopt the younger children and bring the family back together."

"Do you understand these children have a lot of problems? They haven't done well in school so they were sent here to stay," the woman exclaimed.

"We know there are problems, but we'd like the chance to work with them and send them to school," said Momma.

The woman continued, "The orphanage in your town sent a good report on you. We'll do the paper work for the two children here, and I can tell you where the other two girls are."

"That would be wonderful. We would be so thankful if we could have them with us by New Year's," said Papa.

"I'll see what I can do," said the woman.

The trip to the other two orphanages went much the same way. God was going before them answering their prayers and doing miracles.

"New Year's 2004 was another miracle. Seven of the nine brothers and sisters we wanted to find were here celebrating with us," said Papa.

"The adoption of Anastasia [Ahn-ah-sta-SEE-uh], Nikolai [NIK-oh-lie], Tanya [Tah-NEE-ah], and Nanya [Nah-NEE-ah] should be complete by the end of the year," said Momma.

"Let's see," said Sasha. "That's four and Viktoria and Evgenii make six. With Momma and Papa and the three of us kids, that makes eleven in this house. Our house isn't big enough for that many people."

"That's right," said Papa. "I talked with the church. They agree we need to build on to the house and the church. The church is growing, also."

"Can Anastasia go to school with me?" asked Sasha.

"All four children will start to school with you tomorrow," answered Momma.

❊ ❊ ❊

The children worked hard at school, and Momma helped them at home. Many children came, finding a place to belong in their home.

As children joined the family, each child became a part of the team. Their everyday schedule included prayer in the morning and evening. Olga made sure each child studied and completed their daily chores.

❊ ❊ ❊

A few years later, Momma said, "Sasha, Dimitrii is away at school. You are 17, so it's time for you to go away to school, too."

"Momma, I don't want to leave you and Papa. There's so much to do here. Even with Dimitrii and me at school, you still have seven children at home," Sasha replied.

"I'll miss you, Sasha, but you must continue your education," said Momma.

✳ ✳ ✳

With Sasha away at school, Momma still made time to help at the orphanage and invited children to visit their home. She always made them feel like they had a place to belong.

"Ring, ring, ring!"

"Hello, this is Olga."

"I am the director of orphanages. We know you've helped at orphanages over the years and have adopted several children. We trust you and know you care about children," said the director.

"Thank you," said Momma, "I appreciate your kind words."

"I have a special request of you," said the director.

"What is it?" Momma asked.

The director explained, "We have a 13-year-old boy named Velerii [VEL-ee-ree] who continues to run away. His mother died when he was young. The boy doesn't trust anyone. Would you and your husband consider taking him for one month? This boy needs a home like yours to help him."

5
Becoming a Family

Momma told the family about Valerii. They decided to invite Velerii for one month.

"Thank you," said Momma.

✳ ✳ ✳

After a month, Velerii said, "I'd like to stay here."

"It'll be hard work," said Papa. Our family's a team. We work together, pray together, and serve Jesus together."

Papa continued, "We can't give you many riches, but with God you have a great chance in life. We are a family, Momma and I and twelve children."

"I'm glad I'm number twelve," smiled Velerii.

"We're glad too," said Momma and Papa.

What can children do to help?

Pray for:

1. Children who do not have a home.
2. Families who adopt children.
3. A child for your family to love.

Give:

1. Money through your local church or district to assist families who adopt children.
2. Money to the general children's mission offering, "Kids Reaching Kids."

Discussion Questions

1. How could your family include other children?

2. Did Sasha's family make right choices?

3. How do you know when God is speaking?

4. How would you feel if your family wanted to adopt a child?